P9-CFY-103

Dear Mary

for your creative
programming and
hanging in with a
tough job — you have
my heartfelt thanks
and gratitude.

Fondly,

Didi

May 1990

A Token
of
Friendship

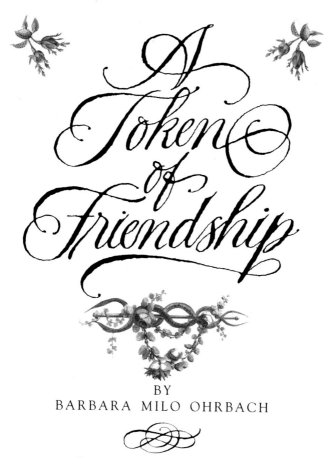

A Token of Friendship

BY
BARBARA MILO OHRBACH

*A collection of sentiments, thoughts,
gift ideas, and recipes for special friends*

CLARKSON N. POTTER, INC./PUBLISHERS

Publisher's Note: This book contains several potpourri recipes, using dried flowers, herbs, and other natural ingredients. Some of these components may cause allergic reactions in some individuals, so reasonable care in preparation is advised.

Copyright © 1987 by Barbara Milo Ohrbach

Published by Clarkson N. Potter, Inc., 201 East 50th Street, New York, New York 10022, and distributed by Crown Publishers, Inc.

CLARKSON N. POTTER, POTTER, and colophon are trademarks of Clarkson N. Potter, Inc.

Manufactured in Japan

Design by Justine Strasberg

Library of Congress Cataloging-in-Publication Data

Ohrbach, Barbara Milo.
A token of friendship.

1. Cookery. 2. Gifts. 3. Friendship—
Quotations, maxims, etc. I. Title.
TX652.037 1987   745.5   87–7000
ISBN 0-517-56657-5
15 14 13 12 11 10

Recipes

To my best friend,
Mel

A token of friendship and thanks to all who
helped on this book, especially—

Everyone at Clarkson N. Potter who worked
so hard with so little time—Carol Southern,
Carolyn Hart, Gretchen Salisbury, Gael Towey,
Rusty Porter, Ann Cahn, and Teresa Nicholas.

Deborah Geltman, for her wonderful advice
and support.

Patti McCarthy, a dear friend, who was there
through it all, baking between quotes.

Tina Strasberg who took all my bits and pieces
and designed something very lovely.

Jutta Buck, of Jutta Buck Antiquarian Books
and Prints, Evelyn Kraus of Ursus Prints,
and Jane Stubbs of Stubbs Prints for graciously
making available to me their wonderful
collections.

And lastly, I wish I could personally thank
each of the exceptional people whose very
special quotes fill these pages.

Introduction

I love everything that's old; old friends,
old times, old manners, old books, old wines.

OLIVER GOLDSMITH

 And, I might add, old thoughts.
For years when I'd come across a
poem or touching quotation I
wanted to remember, I'd jot it down on a scrap
of paper. Weeks or months later I'd find it,
with delight, in an old handbag ready to go to
the thrift shop or in the pocket of a skirt not
worn since last winter. The quotes accumu-
lated, like so many of the old treasures
that I tend to collect.

On the other hand, I like to give things
away—a trait probably acquired from my
mother. No one leaves our house without a
"little something" to take home—a bunch of
herbs, a good book, a new recipe. And I
wouldn't think of visiting someone, particularly
friends or family, without bringing a gift that I
thought they would enjoy.

We all love to share special things with others, and that's why I decided to do this book about friendship. It is a collection of some of my favorite quotations and beautiful old 18th- and 19th-century engravings. I've included delicious and easy recipes and gift ideas, many given to me by my good friends.

I hope you enjoy this book. It is meant to be a gift in itself—a "little something" that you can give to the people you care most about.

Barbara Milo Ohrbach
New York City

My books are friends that never fail me.
THOMAS CARLYLE

 Life is nothing without friendship.
CICERO

When the sun shines on you,
you see your friends.
Friends are the thermometers
by which one may judge
the temperature of our fortunes.
COUNTESS OF BLESSINGTON

1

The heart never becomes wrinkled.

MME. DE SÉVIGNÉ

Sugar Heart Cookies

These cookies make lovely gifts packed into bright red tins and tied with ribbon. Separate each layer with red cellophane.

1 CUP UNSALTED BUTTER
1 CUP SUGAR
2 LARGE EGGS, BEATEN
3½ CUPS FLOUR
¼ TEASPOON SALT

1 TABLESPOON BAKING POWDER
⅓ CUP MILK
2 TEASPOONS VANILLA
RED SUGAR CRYSTALS

✦ Soften butter to room temperature. Place in a bowl and blend in sugar gradually. Add eggs one at a time, beating until mixture is light and fluffy. Set aside.

✦ Sift together flour, salt, and baking powder. Set aside.

✦ Mix milk with vanilla. Set aside.

✦ Stir dry ingredients alternately with milk mixture into creamed egg mixture to form the dough. Chill overnight.

✦ Preheat oven to 400°F. Roll dough ⅛ inch thick on a floured surface and cut with a heart-shaped cookie cutter. Sprinkle with red sugar. Put one inch apart on greased baking sheet.

✦ Bake cookies about 8 minutes or until lightly browned on the bottoms. Cool on racks.

MAKES APPROXIMATELY 4 DOZEN

Business, you know, may bring money,
but friendship hardly ever does.

JANE AUSTEN

Be courteous to all,
but intimate with few,
and let those few be well tried
before you give them your confidence.
True friendship is a plant
of slow growth,
and must undergo
and withstand
the shocks of adversity before it is
entitled to the appellation.

GEORGE WASHINGTON

Music is love in search of a word.

SIDNEY LANIER

Be slow in choosing a friend, slower in changing.

BENJAMIN FRANKLIN

And the song, from beginning to end,
I found in the heart of a friend.

HENRY WADSWORTH LONGFELLOW

A true friend is the greatest of all blessings.

DUC DE LA ROCHEFOUCAULD

I never met a man I didn't like.

WILL ROGERS

There's rosemary, that's for remembrance:
pray you, love, remember.

WILLIAM SHAKESPEARE

Rosemary Reviver

A terrific pick-me-up to use on hot summer days as a skin freshener or splash. A bottle in a guest bathroom is a thoughtful touch.

1 CUP FRESH ROSEMARY
SPRIGS FROM THE
GARDEN, OR 4 OUNCES
DRIED ROSEMARY

2 CUPS WATER
PRETTY JAR OR BOTTLE
AND RIBBON

✦ Boil rosemary in water for several minutes. Let cool.

✦ Pour into a pretty jar or bottle, straining out the sprigs.

✦ Tie a ribbon around the neck of the bottle.

✦ Refrigerate.

MAKES 2 CUPS

If you would be loved, love and be lovable.

BENJAMIN FRANKLIN

An acquaintance that
begins with a compliment
is sure to develop
into a real friendship.

OSCAR WILDE

The better part of one's life consists of his
friendships.

ABRAHAM LINCOLN

If a man does not make
new acquaintances
as he advances through life,
he will soon find himself left alone.
A man, sir, should keep his
friendship in a constant repair.

SAMUEL JOHNSON

There is no possession
more valuable than
a good and faithful friend

SOCRATES

Of all the things
which wisdom provides
to make life entirely happy,
much the greatest
is the possession
of friendship.

EPICURUS

A friend is a person
with whom I may be sincere.
Before him I may think aloud.

RALPH WALDO EMERSON

9

Small cheer and great welcome makes a merry feast.

WILLIAM SHAKESPEARE

Patti's Delicious Dip

This is a wonderful, flavorful dip that can be made a day ahead and brought to the next housewarming or picnic you are invited to. Arrange a flat herb basket with glass tumblers lined with cotton napkins. Fill each glass with a different raw vegetable: baby carrots; French radishes; scallions; yellow pear tomatoes; cucumbers; red, yellow, and green peppers; blanched broccoli and cauliflower.

1 CUP SOUR CREAM
1 CUP MAYONNAISE
⅓ CUP CHOPPED PARSLEY
3 TABLESPOONS CHOPPED CHIVES

1 TABLESPOON WINE VINEGAR
1 CLOVE GARLIC, CRUSHED
¼ TEASPOON SALT
⅛ TEASPOON PEPPER

❧ Combine all the ingredients in a bowl and mix thoroughly.

✘ Cover and refrigerate overnight.

MAKES APPROXIMATELY 2 CUPS

If you have a friend worth loving, love him.
Yes, and let him know that you love him,
ere life's evening tinge his brow with sunset glow.
Why should good words ne'er be said of a friend—
till he is dead?

ANONYMOUS

We have been friends together
In sunshine and shade.

CAROLINE NORTON

Friendship is a strong and habitual inclination
in two persons to promote the good and
happiness of one another.

EUSTACE BUDGELL

For whoever knows how to
return a kindness he has received
must be a friend above all price.

SOPHOCLES

Friendship
is the marriage of the soul.
VOLTAIRE

But every road is rough to me
that has no friend to cheer it.
ELIZABETH SHANE

Fame is the scentless sunflower,
with gaudy crown of gold;
But friendship is the breathing rose,
with sweets in every fold.

OLIVER WENDELL HOLMES

Rose Hip Tea

Herbal teas are delicious and this one, a delicate rose color, is especially refreshing. Packed in pretty containers, they make a very special gift.

1 CUP DRIED ROSE HIPS, FROM THE GARDEN OR STORE BOUGHT

SMALL DECORATIVE TINS AND LABELS

Crush rose hips finely with a mortar and pestle. You should have 12 teaspoons.

Spoon rose hips into small tin containers with tops.

Tie a label on each tin that says, "Place one teaspoonful of rose hips in a cup. Add boiling water and steep for 3 to 5 minutes. Enjoy!" Then add your favorite friendship quote.

MAKES 12 CUPS OF TEA

Friendship is a word
the very sight of which in print
makes the heart warm.

AUGUSTINE BIRRELL

There was nothing remote or mysterious here—
only something private.
The only secret was the ancient communication
between two people.

EUDORA WELTY

The thread of our life would be dark,
Heaven knows!
If it were not with friendship and love intertwin'd.

THOMAS MOORE

Love is best.

ROBERT BROWNING

Thou wert my guide, philosopher and friend.

ALEXANDER POPE

Each friend represents a world in us,
a world possibly not born until they arrive,
and it is only by this meeting
that a new world is born.

ANAÏS NIN

All who would win joy, must share it;
happiness was born a twin.

LORD BYRON

The best smell is bread, the best saver salt,
the best love that of children.

GEORGE HERBERT

Spicy Banana Bread

Friends and friends' children love when you bring this over—it can be eaten for breakfast, afternoon tea, or dessert.

2 CUPS FLOUR
1 TEASPOON BAKING SODA
½ TEASPOON SALT
½ TEASPOON CINNAMON
¼ TEASPOON NUTMEG
¼ TEASPOON CLOVES
½ CUP UNSALTED BUTTER

1 CUP SUGAR
2 EGGS
1 CUP MASHED BANANAS
¼ CUP ORANGE JUICE
1 CUP CHOPPED WALNUTS
1 TEASPOON VANILLA

✦ Preheat oven to 350°F. Grease and flour a 9-x-5-x-3-inch loaf pan. Soften butter to room temperature.

✦ Sift flour with baking soda, salt, and spices.

✦ Cream butter and gradually add sugar, beating until the mixture is light and fluffy.

✦ Beat in eggs, one at a time. Add sifted dry ingredients alternately with mashed bananas and orange juice, stirring only to blend.

✦ Fold in nuts and vanilla.

✦ Pour batter into greased loaf pan and bake one hour. Let cool 30 minutes in pan.

MAKES ONE LOAF

A friend is,
as it were,
a second self.

CICERO

. . . being with you is like
walking on a very clear morning—
definitely the sensation
of belonging there.

E. B. WHITE

Our affections are our life.
We live by them;
they supply our warmth.

WILLIAM ELLERY CHANNING

He liked to like people;
therefore people liked him.

MARK TWAIN

20

True happiness consists
not in the multitude of friends,
But in the worth and choice.

BEN JONSON

Promises may get friends,
but it is performance
that must nurse and keep them.

OWEN FELLTHAM

A friend should bear his friend's infirmities.

WILLIAM SHAKESPEARE

Man strives for glory, honor, fame,
That all the world may know his name.
Amasses wealth by brain and hand;
Becomes a power in the land.
But when he nears the end of life
And looks back o'er the years of strife,
He finds that happiness depends
On none of these, but love of friends.

ANONYMOUS

21

I *find friendship to be like wine,*
raw when new, ripened with age,
the true old man's milk
and restorative cordial.

THOMAS JEFFERSON

Ruby Cordial

With *its bright red color this is a festive gift to bring to friends at Christmastime. Pour into beautiful bottles and tie the necks with wide green ribbons and a sprig of holly or juniper.*

1½ CUPS WHOLE, FRESH
    CRANBERRIES
  2 CUPS VODKA
  2 CUPS SUGAR

1 ORANGE JUICE
  BOTTLE, QUART SIZE
  DECORATIVE GLASS
  BOTTLES

✦ Crush cranberries in a bowl with a metal spoon.

✦ Add vodka and sugar.

✦ Pour into juice bottle and let sit for about a month. Stir every 10 days to dissolve sugar.

✦ Pour into decorative bottles, straining out cranberries.

MAKES 24 OUNCES

Be a friend to yourself, and others will.

Love demands infinitely less than friendship.

GEORGE JEAN NATHAN

That best portion of a good man's life,
His little, nameless, unremembered acts
Of kindness and of love.

WILLIAM WORDSWORTH

A friend is a present which you give yourself.

ROBERT LOUIS STEVENSON

Friendship is love with understanding.

ANCIENT PROVERB

The only way
to have a friend
is to be one.

RALPH WALDO EMERSON

A real friend is one who walks in
when the rest of the world walks out.

WALTER WINCHELL

*F*riendship is a union of spirits, a marriage
of hearts, and the bond thereof virtue.

WILLIAM PENN

Wedding Lavender

This is a fragrant
*alternative to the rice traditionally thrown at the
bride and groom.*

12 OUNCES DRIED
   LAVENDER FLOWERS,
   FROM THE GARDEN
   OR STORE BOUGHT

TULLE FABRIC
LAVENDER SATIN
RIBBON

❧ Sew up little tulle bags, approximately 5
inches high by 4 inches wide on three sides;
leave ¼-inch seam allowance.

❧ Fill the bags with about one ounce of dry
fragrant lavender.

❧ Tie with lavender satin ribbons and give
one bag to each guest.

❧ As the bride and groom leave, throw the
lavender as you would rice.

MAKES ENOUGH TO FILL ONE DOZEN BAGS

The happiest moments my heart knows
are those in which it is pouring forth
its affections to a few esteemed characters.

THOMAS JEFFERSON

Time draweth wrinkles in a fair face,
but addeth fresh colors to a fast friend,
which neither heat, nor cold,
nor misery, nor place,
nor destiny, can alter or diminish.

JOHN LYLY

Above our life we love a steadfast friend.

CHRISTOPHER MARLOWE

The loss of a beloved deserving friend
is the hardest trial of philosophy.

MARY WORTLEY MONTAGUE

The test of friendship is assistance in adversity,
and that, too, unconditional assistance.

MAHATMA GANDHI

Happiness seems made to be shared.

JEAN RACINE

The bird a nest, the spider a web,
man friendship.

WILLIAM BLAKE

Birdseed Picnic

This is a gift for our
friends, the birds, and it is also a nice gift for
nature-minded friends. This mixture will attract
most varieties, including cardinals, chickadees,
blue jays, gold and purple finches, and sparrows.

8 OUNCES STRIPED
   SUNFLOWER SEEDS
6 OUNCES OIL SUN-
   FLOWER SEEDS
14 OUNCES SMALL
   CHICK CORN

6 OUNCES MILLET
2 OUNCES THISTLE
4 OUNCES PEANUT
   HEARTS

✦ Mix all the ingredients together in a bowl.
✦ Divide into small paper bags.
✦ Tie each bag with ribbon or green garden
twine.

MAKES 2½ POUNDS BIRD-FEED MIXTURE

There's nothing worth the wear of winning,
But laughter and the love of friends.

HILLAIRE BELLOC

Guard within yourself that treasure, kindness.
Know how to give without hesitation,
how to lose without regret,
how to acquire without meanness.
Know how to replace in your heart,
by the happiness of those you love,
the happiness that may be wanting to yourself.

GEORGE SAND

Love must be learned,
and learned again and again;
there is no end to it.

KATHERINE ANNE PORTER

There was a definite process
by which one made people into friends,
and it involved talking to them and
listening to them for hours at a time.

REBECCA WEST

Let me live in a house
by the side of the road
and be a friend to man.

SAM WALTER FOSS

A friend in need is a friend indeed.

ENGLISH PROVERB

I no doubt deserved my enemies,
but I don't believe I deserved my friends.

WALT WHITMAN

A man must get friends
as he would get food and drink for
nourishment and sustenance.
RANDOLPH SILLIMAN BOURNE

Old-Fashioned Pound Cake

There's nothing quite like a piece of cozy pound cake to lift your spirits. This is an especially nice gift for someone who's just come home from the hospital or an elderly friend.

1 CUP UNSALTED BUTTER

2 CUPS SUGAR

3 EGGS, BEATEN

2 CUPS UNBLEACHED FLOUR

1 TABLESPOON BAKING POWDER

1 TEASPOON BAKING SODA

½ TEASPOON SALT

2 CUPS SOUR CREAM

1 TABLESPOON VANILLA

♦ Preheat oven to 350°F. and grease a 10-inch bundt pan. Allow butter to soften.

♦ Using an electric mixer, cream butter until fluffy and light yellow. Slowly add sugar and then eggs one at a time, beating continuously.

♦ Sift together flour, baking powder, soda, and salt.

♦ Stir in small amounts of flour mixture alternately with sour cream. Add vanilla.

♦ Pour batter into bundt pan and bake 45 to 60 minutes until cake tester comes out clean.

MAKES 8 TO 10 SERVINGS

Hold a true friend with both your hands.

A friend may well be reckoned the masterpiece
of nature.

RALPH WALDO EMERSON

Like everyone else
I feel the need of relations and friendship,
of affection, of friendly intercourse,
and I am not made of stone or iron,
so I cannot miss these things without feeling,
as does any other intelligent man,
a void and deep need.
I tell you this to let you know
how much good your visit has done me.

VINCENT VAN GOGH

For there is no friend like a sister
In calm or stormy weather;
To cheer one on the tedious way,
To fetch one if one goes astray,
To lift one if one totters down,
To strengthen whilst one stands.

CHRISTINA ROSSETTI

I would be friends with you
and have your love.

WILLIAM SHAKESPEARE

Traveling in the company
of those we love is home in motion.

LEIGH HUNT

There is a magic in
the memory of schoolboy friendships;
it softens the heart, and
even affects the nervous system
of those who have no heart.

BENJAMIN DISRAELI

The beauty of the house is order,
The blessing of the house is contentment;
The glory of the house is hospitality.

HOUSE BLESSING

Quick Spicy Sachet

T*his is a wonderful gift for
a friend who loves to cook. The sachet scents the
kitchen quickly and covers up strong cooking
odors. Each sachet can be used several times.*

2 OUNCES WHOLE
  CLOVES
1 OUNCE BAY LEAVES
½ OUNCE CRUSHED
  NUTMEG
½ OUNCE CRUSHED
  GINGER

1 OUNCE BROKEN
  CINNAMON STICKS
1 OUNCE ORANGE PEEL
  MUSLIN FABRIC
  STRING

✦ Mix all the herbs and spices in a bowl.
Crush nutmeg and ginger gently with a
hammer.

✦ Sew up little muslin bags approximately 5
inches high by 4 inches wide on three sides;
leave ¼-inch seam allowance. Fill the bags and
tie with string.

✦ Fill a saucepan with water and place the
sachet in the pan. As the water begins to boil,
turn off. The scent will fill the room, and if the
breeze is right, the rest of the house as well.

MAKES ENOUGH TO FILL 6 BAGS

Those who love deeply never grow old;
they may die of old age, but they die young.

SIR ARTHUR WING PINERO

Reprove a friend in secret,
but praise him before others.

LEONARDO DA VINCI

A true friend unbosoms freely,
advises justly, assists readily,
adventures boldly, takes all patiently,
defends courageously, and continues
a friend unchangeably.

WILLIAM PENN

Silences make the real
conversations between friends.
Not the saying but the never
needing to say is what counts.
ANONYMOUS

Friendship's the wine of life.
EDWARD YOUNG

Nature never did betray
the heart that loved her.
WILLIAM WORDSWORTH

Friends, books, a cheerful heart,
and conscience clear are the most
choice companions we have here.

WILLIAM MATHER

Herb Leaf Bookmark

Pressed flowers or leaves can be evocative remembrances of a special summer day. Make them into bookmarks and add to books that you give as presents for Christmas—a thoughtful dividend.

✦ Take some of your favorite flattish-type herb leaves—such as costmary, sage, sweet woodruff, lemon verbena, or lemon balm—and flatten between two blotter papers. Place between the pages of a heavy book or in a flower press. Remove in several days when the leaves are dry.

✦ If desired, paint the leaves with clear nail polish to preserve them.

✦ Cut pieces of interesting paper—marbleized or rice paper, for instance—to bookmark size (7 inches long by 2 inches wide) and glue each leaf to the paper with rubber cement.

Good company in a journey makes the way
to seem the shorter.

IZAAK WALTON

I want a warm and faithful friend,
To cheer the adverse hour;
Who ne'er to flatter will descend,
Not bend the knee to power.
A friend to chide me when I'm wrong,
My inmost soul to see;
And that my friendship prove as strong
To him as his to me.

JOHN QUINCY ADAMS

 Friendship is always
a sweet responsibility,
never an opportunity.

KAHLIL GIBRAN

The most I can do for my friend
is simply be his friend.

HENRY DAVID THOREAU

Friendship consists in forgetting what one gives
and remembering what one receives.

ALEXANDRE DUMAS THE YOUNGER

The happiest moments of my life have been the
few which I have passed at home in the bosom
of my family.

THOMAS JEFFERSON

Friendship is unnecessary,
like philosophy, like art . . .
It has no survival value;
rather it is one of those things
that give value to survival.

C. S. LEWIS

Wishing to be friends is quick work,
but friendship is a slow-ripening fruit.

ARISTOTLE

Orange Peel Potpourri

$This$ is a wonderfully easy and very fragrant scent idea you can make continuously all year long. Every time you eat an orange, save the peel. If you'd like to do it all at once, here is the recipe.

8 ORANGES   4 OUNCES CLOVES

❧ Peel the oranges and break the peel into rough pieces approximately 1-inch square.

❧ Insert 1 to 3 whole cloves into each piece of peel.

❧ Set to dry in a flat basket or box.

❧ When dry, scoop the pieces of clove-studded orange peel into a pretty bowl and set on a side table to scent an area in a room. Or fill an old basket with the peel, tie with a wide ribbon, and bring as a gift to a friend.

MAKES 1 SMALL BOWL OR BASKET

Friendship is the most worthy of human ties.
A man loves his friend's soul, and
to do that he must have a soul himself.

GEORGES LOUIS LECLERC DE BUFFON

Friendship improves happiness,
and abates misery, by doubling our joy,
and dividing our grief.

JOSEPH ADDISON

It is great to have friends
when one is young,
but indeed it is still more so
when you are getting old.
When we are young,
friends are, like everything else,
a matter of course.
In the old days we know
what it means to have them.

EDVARD GRIEG

Friendship is almost always
the union of a part of one mind
with a part of another;
people are friends in spots.

GEORGE SANTAYANA

Love me please; I love you;
I can bear to be your friend.

EDNA ST. VINCENT MILLAY

The best moments of a visit
are those which again and again
postpone its close.

JEAN PAUL RICHTER

Welcome Herb Wreath

It's fun to welcome guests to
your house with a beautiful herbal wreath
hanging over a mirror in the front hall or foyer.
This wreath has removable bunches that each
guest may take home as a fragrant remembrance
as they leave.

❦ Take 3 or 4 dried sprigs of different herbs,
such as bay leaves, artemisia, lavender,
rosemary, thyme, sage, germander, or box, for
example, and tie together in a pretty bunch
with a rubber band. Then tie and bow with
your favorite ½-inch-wide ribbon. Tartan plaid
would be beautiful at Christmastime, pale
pastels in spring.

❦ Using florist pins, pin the ribboned bunches
onto a 10-inch straw wreath form in the same
direction. The pins are easily removable so
each guest can take one.

F*riendship with oneself is all-important
because without it one cannot be friends
with anyone else in the world.*

ELEANOR ROOSEVELT

W*hat is thine is mine, and all mine is thine.*

PLAUTUS

T*o God, thy country, and thy friend be true.*

HENRY VAUGHAN

F*riendship is a sheltering tree.*

SAMUEL TAYLOR COLERIDGE

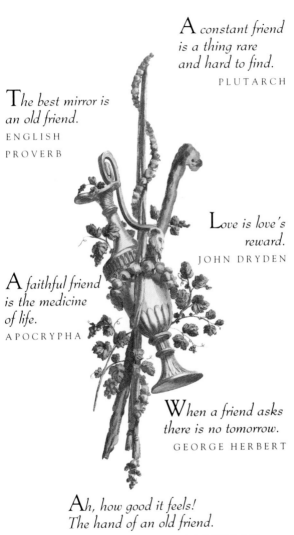

A constant friend
is a thing rare
and hard to find.
PLUTARCH

The best mirror is
an old friend.
ENGLISH
PROVERB

Love is love's
reward.
JOHN DRYDEN

A faithful friend
is the medicine
of life.
APOCRYPHA

When a friend asks
there is no tomorrow.
GEORGE HERBERT

Ah, how good it feels!
The hand of an old friend.
HENRY WADSWORTH LONGFELLOW

53

While the pot boils, friendship blooms.

A. B. CHEALES

Chicken Soup

This recipe is like a
dependable old friend. It is also simple, warm,
and reassuring. Why don't you make it to bring to
one of your old friends on a cold winter day?

1 4-POUND CHICKEN
3 QUARTS COLD WATER
1 PARSNIP, PEELED
2 CARROTS, PEELED
1 STALK CELERY
1 LARGE ONION
1 CLOVE GARLIC

6 SPRIGS PARSLEY, TIED
1 TEASPOON SALT
SEVERAL WHOLE
PEPPERCORNS

✦ Wash the whole chicken thoroughly, then
cut into parts.

✦ Place the chicken in a large pot and cover
with the water. Bring to a boil, approximately
30 minutes.

✖ Skim the fat off the top.

✦ Add the remaining ingredients, cover and
simmer slowly for about 2½ hours or until
chicken is tender.

✖ Remove vegetables and set chicken aside
for other uses.

MAKES ABOUT 2 QUARTS

The only thing to do
is to hug one's friends tight
and do one's job.

EDITH WHARTON